Starting Out

14 Week Bible Study For New Christians

Kevin Simington

Aaron Wardle

Wangaratta Baptist Publishing

Starting Out

CONTENTS

About These Studies — 2

1. Jesus Our Saviour — 4
2. Faith — 12
3. Repentance — 20
4. Baptism — 28
5. The Holy Spirit — 36
6. The Bible - God's Word — 44
7. Prayer — 52
8. The Church — 60
9. Overcoming Temptation — 68
10. Sharing Your Faith — 76
11. Worshiping God — 84
12. Serving God — 92

CONTENTS

13 | Giving To God 100

14 | The Lord's Supper 108

Introduction: A New Begining

Deciding to accept Jesus Christ as your Lord and Saviour is the most important and life changing decision you will ever make! If you truly turn to Him in faith and repentance you become a child of God - a dearly loved member of His family. You may not feel any different but when you accept Jesus into your life a truly miraculous change takes place within you. The Bible says you are "born again" (John 3:7). Your spirit, which until now has been dead towards God, is brought to life by God's Holy Spirit who comes to dwell within you. You literally become a "new creation" (2 Corinthians 5:17).

In God's eyes the old you is gone and a new you has been created - created to be just like Jesus. It may take some time for this new you to become apparent. In fact the process of making this internal change an external reality will go on for the rest of your life! But God sees the new you already, and He accepts you and loves you as His child.

As a child of God you can be completely assured that your sins have been forgiven and that God has already prepared a place for you in heaven. You can be assured that God will hear you and answer your prayers and that He has a wonderful purpose for your life, revealed in His Word, the Bible.

There is nothing you have done to deserve this: it is all a wonderful gift from God, paid for by the death and resurrection of Jesus.

You can expect that the devil will try to make you doubt what God has done in your life. This is common. When this happens you simply need to trust Jesus' words: "I tell you the truth, whoever hears my words and believes Him who sent me has eternal life and will not be condemned; he has crossed over from death to life" (John 5:24).

If you have truly turned to Jesus in faith and repentance, then this promise is true for you!

WHAT A WONDERFUL NEW BEGINNING.

About These Studies

AIM

These studies have been designed to help you as you start out in the Christian journey. They will help you in three ways:

1. They will show you how a person becomes a Christian and helps you know for certain whether this has happened in your life.
2. They will teach you some very important principles that God wants you to know about living the Christian life.
3. They will help you to begin to put these principles into action.

HOW TO USE THESE STUDIES

There are 14 weekly studies. Each study is divided into 7 daily portions. Each day you will have a Bible passage to look up and some questions to answer which will help you think about the passage and discover what it is saying. Try to write down an answer for each question. There may be some questions that you can't answer, simply leave these blank and your discipler or teacher will help you with them when you meet.

Ideally you should have someone to meet with you each week to discuss the study you have just done, answer your questions and talk with you about how you are going in your Christian life.

LOOKING UP BIBLE PASSAGES.

Each Bible passage in the studies is indicated by a name and then some numbers separated by a colon. These indicate the name of the book in the Bible, the chapter, and the verses. For instance:

"John 3:1-16" refers to the book of John, chapter 3, verses 1 to 16.

> BOOKS: You can find these by looking up the index at the front of your Bible.
>
> CHAPTERS: These are indicated by the large numbers interspersed throughout the books.
>
> VERSES: These are indicated by the small numbers at the beginning of most sentences in the Bible.

HAVING A DAILY QUIET TIME

These studies are designed to help you have a daily time of Bible reading and prayer. Christians often refer to this as a "Quiet Time". This is time when you draw near to God in prayer and receive from Him spiritual nourishment as He speaks to you through the words of the Bible. A daily quiet time is essential for your growth and health as a Christian.

1. **Choose a Specific Time**: It is much easier to have a daily quiet time if you have it at the same time every day. Write the time that best suits you here: _____

2. **Choose a Specific Place**: Choosing a location that is free from noise or interruption is also important. What is the best place for you? _____

3. **Have a Bible and pen handy**: Use a modern translation of the Bible - it will be easier to understand. Your discipler or teacher can help you with this.

4. **Begin with Prayer**: Ask God to help you concentrate and to understand what He is saying in the Bible passage. Ask Him to Speak personally to you as you read and pray.

5. **Read the passage several times**: By the 2nd or 3rd time you will start to see things in the passage that you didn't at first.

6. **Think**: Spend time asking yourself: "What is it really saying? What does it mean for me? Is there something here for me to do? Something new to consider? Some change I need to make in my life?

7. **Pray**: Ask God to help you remember and put into practice what you have learnt. Many Christians find the ACTS "formula" of prayer helpful:

Adoration: Praise God for His greatness and love

Confessions: Admitting your sins and asking for forgiveness.

Thanksgiving: Thanking God for what He has done for you.

Supplication: Making requests for yourself and others.

Sometimes in these studies you are reminded to pray - more often you are not. Prayer should be a part of every quiet time, whether the studies specifically mention it or not.

8. **Remember** what you have learnt as you go through your day.

1

Jesus Our Saviour

The Bible tells us that Jesus is the son of God, and that together with God the Father and God the Holy Spirit, He is the creator of the universe. About 2000 year ago He left heaven and came to earth as a human being. He allowed Himself to be put to death on a cross to pay for the sins of the world - to be punished in our place - so that all people could have a chance to be forgiven. What amazing Love!

STARTING OUT

DAY 1 - Read Colossians 1:15-23

This passage is speaking about Jesus. What 2 things does verse 15 tell us about Him?

_____
_____
_____

Verse 19 explains the first of these truths a little more. What is this really saying about Jesus? (See John 1:1).

_____
_____
_____

Verses 16-17 explain the second important truth about Jesus. Why do you think He is called "the firstborn over all creation"?

_____
_____
_____

What authority does this give Him over us? (verse 18).

_____
_____
_____

DAY 2 - Read Colossians 1:15-23 again

What has Jesus done for us? (verse 20)
_____
_____
_____

Why was this necessary? (verse 21)
_____
_____
_____

Who do you think verse 21 applies to?
_____
_____
_____

What is the only thing that can make us "holy" (acceptable) to God? (verse 22)
_____
_____
_____

DAY 3 - Read Isaiah 59:1-13

This passage describes a serious problem we all have: SIN. Sin is rebellion against God. It is a spiritual sickness that every person has. List the specific sins this passage mentions:

_____
_____
_____

Verse 13 describes the essence of sin (from which all individual sins come). What is it?

_____
_____
_____

How has this affected our relationship with God?

_____
_____
_____

Do you think there are any people who aren't sinners? (See Romans 3:23)

_____
_____
_____

Spend time confessing to God the ways you rebel against Him. Ask for forgiveness through the death of Jesus for you.

DAY 4 - Read 1 Peter 2:21-25

This passage tells us what happened when Jesus died on the cross. Apart from the nails in his hands and feet, what else happened in his body as He hung on the cross? (verse 24)

_____
_____
_____

What do you think this means?

_____
_____
_____

What other suffering did Jesus endure? (verse 23)

_____
_____
_____

Who did He do this for? (verse 21)

_____
_____
_____

Why did He do this? (verses 24-25)

_____
_____
_____

DAY 5 - Read Romans 5:1-10

What 5 things has the death of Jesus done for us?

Verse 1:
Verse 1:
Verse 2:
Verse 10:
Verse 10:

What makes us acceptable to God? (verse 9)
_____
_____
_____

What will this rescue us from? (verse 9)
_____
_____
_____

What must we have to receive this? (verse 1)
_____
_____
_____

DAY 6 - Read John 14:1-9

This is Jesus speaking. What "place" is He speaking about in verses 1-4?
___
___
___

Why does He say He was going back there?
___
___
___

Jesus claimed 3 things about Himself in verse 6. What do you think each one means?

    "the way":
    "the truth":
    "the life":

What is Jesus claiming in the second half of verse 6?
___
___
___

DAY 7 - PERSONAL REFLECTION

Day 7 of each study will be set aside as a time for personal reflection. Read back over the things you have learnt this week. Write down here any questions you have about any of the things you have studied. Your discipler will help to answer these and any other questions you have about the Christian faith.

Questions I have from this week:
_____
_____
_____
_____
_____
_____
_____
_____
_____
_____

What is the most important thing you have learned this week?
_____
_____
_____
_____
_____
_____
_____

2

Faith

Jesus died for the sins of the whole world. He rose from the dead to offer us all forgiveness and a place in His kingdom. He offers this as a FREE GIFT. In order to receive this free gift of eternal life we need FAITH.

Faith is more than just belief. It is loving and trusting Jesus with your whole heart and seeking to follow Him with your whole life. True Biblical faith is not a passive or intellectual thing. It is life-changing.

STARTING OUT

DAY 1 - Read Romans 3:9-26

In this passage "righteousness" means right with God or acceptable to God, and "justified" means treated as if I had never sinned.

What are verses 9-18 basically saying about all people?

_____
_____
_____

What is clearly impossible for us to do? (verse 20)

_____
_____
_____

What is the only way we can be made "righteous"? (verse 22)

_____
_____
_____

Can we do anything to earn or deserve this? (verses 22-23)

_____
_____
_____

Why or Why not?

_____
_____
_____

| 13 |

DAY 2 - Read Romans 3:9-26 again

How is Jesus described in verse 25? What does this mean?

_____
_____
_____

In what must we have faith, in order to be saved? (verse 25)

_____
_____
_____

What does this mean?

_____
_____
_____

Who are the ONLY ones who will be justified by God? (verse 26)

_____
_____
_____

DAY 3 - Read Ephesians 2:1-10

In this passage "grace" means underserved gift or favour from God.

From verses 4 and 7, list the words used to describe how God has treated us:

Vs. 4: _____   Vs. 7: _____
Vs. 4: _____   Vs. 7: _____

According to verse 8 we are saved:

By .... Through ....

What does "not by works" mean? (verse 9)

_____
_____
_____

DAY 4 - Read 1 John 5:9-12

[Note: 1 John is different to John - It is near the end of the New Testament]

Who gives eternal life? (verse 11)
___
___
___

When does He give it to you: Now or when you die? (verse 11)
___
___
___

Where is this eternal life found? (verse 11)
___
___
___

Who has eternal Life? (verse 12)
___
___
___

Who does not have eternal life? (verse 12)
___
___
___

DAY 5 - Read John 5:24-28

According to verse 24, what 3 things result from hearing and believing in Jesus?

       PRESENT: _____
       FUTURE: _____
       PAST: _____

Why does this verse seem to say that we already have eternal life? What does Jesus mean?

_____
_____
_____

What promise are we given in verse 25?

_____
_____
_____

DAY 6 - Read John 3:35-36

Who is the "SON"?

_____
_____
_____

What has God done for Him? (verse 35) Explain:

_____
_____
_____

Who has eternal life?

_____
_____
_____

Who does not?

_____
_____
_____

What happens to those who reject Jesus?

_____
_____
_____

DAY 7 - PERSONAL REFLECTION

Write down any questions you have about faith:

_____
_____
_____
_____
_____
_____

Faith involves 2 things. Firstly it means BELIEVING. Write down here what you believe about:

WHO JESUS IS:

_____
_____
_____

WHAT HE DID FOR YOU:

_____
_____
_____

Secondly, faith also means TRUSTING. To have faith in Jesus you need to trust that He died on the cross to forgive YOU, and that He can give you a place in heaven. Are you trusting in Jesus or yourself to get to heaven? Here is a good test: Suppose you died tonight, and God said to you: "Why should I let you into heaven?" What would you say?

_____
_____
_____
_____

3

Repentance

God has made His Son Jesus the ruler of the universe. God now calls all people to repent and submit to Jesus as their "Lord" (master). Repentance means changing the direction of your life. It means deciding to live to serve and obey Jesus instead of living to please yourself.

In this study we will see that faith and repentance go hand in hand. Faith is of no value unless it results in a change in the way you live.

DAY 1 - Read James 2:14-19

What should go "hand in hand" with faith in Jesus?

_____
_____
_____

What sorts of actions should this include?

_____
_____
_____

In verse 14 the question is asked "can faith without works save someone?" What answer is given?

_____
_____
_____

Ask yourself: "Has my faith in Jesus resulted in a real change in my life?" List here any things you can think of that have changed:

_____
_____
_____

List some areas of your life that you know you still have to change:

_____
_____
_____

Ask God now to help you change.

Day 2 - Read Acts 3:17-21

Read verse 19. What do you think we are meant to turn from?
_____
_____
_____

What kinds of things would this include?
_____
_____
_____

Who are we turning to? What does this mean?
_____
_____
_____

What 2 things will happen if we do? (verse 19)
_____
_____
_____

Read Acts 17:29-31 Who does God call to repent?
_____
_____
_____

Why should we repent? (verse 31)
_____
_____
_____

DAY 3 - Read John 14:23-24

What should be our motive for obeying Jesus?

___

Is it possible to love Jesus and not want to obey Him?

___

What will God (and Jesus) do if you love and obey Jesus? (verse 23)

___

What does this mean?

___

DAY 4 - Read Ezekiel 18:30-32

What are we commanded to turn away from?
_____
_____
_____

What kind of things will this include? (Give examples).
_____
_____
_____

What do you think "a new heart and a new spirit" means?
_____
_____
_____

Can we do this ourselves? How does it happen?
_____
_____
_____

What does repentance bring? (verse 32)
_____
_____
_____

What will happen to those who don't repent?
_____
_____
_____

DAY 5 - Read Psalm 51

Read verses 3 to 5. Repentance involves admitting your sins and confessing them to God. Write down here some of the ways you know that you have rebelled against God:

_____
_____
_____

Read verses 1, 2, 7, and 9. Repentance also means asking for forgiveness. Spend some time now asking God's forgiveness for the things you have listed and for any other area you can think of.

Read verses 10-17. Repentance also means deciding to change with God's help. Pray now, thanking God for the way He has already started to change you from the inside. Pray for His continued help.

DAY 6 - Read 1 John 1:7-9

Do you think a person can ever reach the point where they never sin? (verse 8)
_____
_____
_____

How then is it possible to be friends with God? (verse 7b)
_____
_____

[Note: verse 7b refers to the second half of the verse]

What must we do continually? (verse 9)
_____
_____
_____

What will God do if we do this? (verse 9)
_____
_____
_____

Day 7 - PERSONAL REFLECTION

We have seen that a Christian is someone who responds to Jesus in faith and repentance.

FAITH: Believe and trust that Jesus is the Son of God and that He died and rose again to forgive your sins.
REPENTANCE: Turn from living life your own way, to follow and obey Jesus.

When we do these 2 things we are accepting Jesus Christ as our Lord and Saviour. Have you done this yet?
_____
_____
_____

You might like to pray this prayer to accept Jesus for the first time, or to confirm what you have already done:
"Dear God, I admit that I am a sinner. I do not deserve your gift of eternal life. I have rebelled against You in thought, word, and deed, sometimes consciously, sometimes without realising it. I am sorry and ask you to forgive me. Thank you for sending your son Jesus to die for my sins. Thank you that He rose from the dead to offer me new life. I accept Him now to be my Lord and Saviour, and I pledge my life to follow and serve Him. AMEN"

Read John 1:12 now, and thank God for making you His child.

4

Baptism

Jesus has commanded that everyone who accepts Him - who becomes His disciple - should be baptised. The word "baptism" refers to the physical act of being immersed completely under water as a symbol that you have been washed clean by Jesus, and that the old life has gone and a new life with God has come. According to the Bible, baptism should occur AFTER someone has become a disciple of Jesus.

DAY 1 - Read Acts 2:38-41

These are the words at the end of the first sermon in the early church. What 2 things are people commanded to do if they want to follow Jesus?

Why were they told to do these 2 things? (verse 38)

How many people were baptised on this occasion? (verse 41)

How soon after hearing this message were they baptised? (verse 41)

Were they baptised before or after they believed?

DAY 2 - Read Matthew 28:16-20

These are the last words of Jesus before He left earth. What 3 things did He command His followers to do?

1. (verse 19)
___
___
___

2. (verse 19)
___
___
___

3. (verse 20)
___
___
___

Notice the order of events. Should a person be baptised before or after becoming a disciple of Jesus?
___
___
___

What promise did He give us? (verse 20)
___
___
___

DAY 3 - Read Romans 6:1-7

When you become a Christian your old way of life is finished. How does baptism by immersion show this? (verse 3)

_____
_____
_____

When you become a Christian, you start to live a new life. How does baptism by immersion show this? (verse 4)

_____
_____
_____

In what way is baptism by immersion a symbol of the resurrection of Jesus?

_____
_____
_____

What does baptism symbolise about the new life of a Christian? (verse 5)

_____
_____
_____

DAY 4 - Read 1 Corinthians 12:12-28

What are we baptised into?
_____
_____
_____

What is another name for this body? (verses 27-28)
_____
_____
_____

What does it mean to be "baptised into" this body?
_____
_____
_____

Water baptism is an outward symbol of being spiritually baptised into this body. Who does this spiritual baptism? (verse 13)
_____
_____
_____

DAY 5 - Read Matthew 3:13-17

Baptism is a symbol of leaving the old sinful life behind and starting a new life with God's forgiveness.

Do you think Jesus needed to do this?

Why or why not?

Why do you think Jesus was baptised?

What does this imply about baptism for us?

DAY 6 - Read 2 Corinthians 5:15-18

Baptism symbolises that a wonderful change has taken place in your life. This passage talks about that change.

What do you become if you are "in Christ"? (verse 17)
_____
_____
_____

What is the "old" that goes?
_____
_____
_____

What is the "new" that comes?
_____
_____
_____

Who makes this happen? (verse 18)
_____
_____
_____

In what way do you think baptism symbolises this?
_____
_____
_____

DAY 7 - PERSONAL REFLECTION

Write down any questions you have about baptism:

_____
_____
_____
_____
_____
_____
_____
_____
_____
_____
_____

Write down any reasons why you shouldn't be baptised or why you don't want to be baptised:

_____
_____
_____
_____
_____
_____
_____
_____
_____
_____
_____
_____

5

The Holy Spirit

The Holy Spirit is a part of God in the same way that Jesus is. The Bible tells us that the Holy Spirit comes to live within us when we accept Jesus Christ as our Lord and Saviour. It is the Holy Spirit who enables us to be "born again" as a child of God and who empowers us to live the Christian life. Every Christian has the Holy Spirit. It is our lifelong job to learn to obey the Holy spirit as He tries to make us more like Jesus.

DAY 1 - Read John 3:3-8

What does this passage say the Holy Spirit does for us?
_____
_____
_____

What do you think it means to be "born again"?
_____
_____
_____

Why do you think we need to be born again?
_____
_____
_____

Is this something we can do ourselves?
_____
_____
_____

DAY 2 - Read John 14:15-18

What name is the Holy Spirit given in verse 16?
_____
_____
_____

Why do you think He is given this name?
_____
_____
_____

What name is the Holy Spirit given in verse 17?
_____
_____
_____

Why do you think He is given this name?
_____
_____
_____

Where is the Holy Spirit? (verse 17)
_____
_____
_____

How long will the Holy Spirit stay with you? (verse 16)
_____
_____
_____

DAY 3 - Read John 16:5-8 and 12-15

Is it better for us to have Jesus with us or the Holy Spirit?
___

Why?
___

What does the Holy Spirit do for us? (verses 13-14)
___

How do you think He does this?
___

DAY 4 - Read Romans 8:9-17

Who has the Holy Spirit? (verse 9)
_____
_____
_____

What did the Holy Spirit do for Jesus? (verse 11)
_____
_____
_____

What kind of "life" do you think He can give us? (verse 11)
_____
_____
_____

What else will the Holy Spirit do for us? (verse 13)
_____
_____
_____

DAY 5 - Read Galatians 5:16-26

What 2 things are at war within us? (verses 16-17)

_____
_____
_____

Who decides which of these will win: The Holy Spirit or us?

_____
_____
_____

What do you think it means to "live by the Spirit"? (verse 16)

_____
_____
_____

Read through the acts of the sinful nature listed in verses 19-21. Spend some time considering which ones you have most trouble with. Pray now for God's Spirit to help you overcome these tendencies.

DAY 6 - Read Galatians 5:16-26 again

List the 9 fruit of the Spirit it mentioned in verses 22-23, and explain each one in your own words:

1:_____

2:_____

3:_____

4:_____

5:_____

6:_____

7:_____

8:_____

9:_____

Read verse 25. It is important to realise that, like physical fruit, this fruit will take time to grow. It will not appear in your life overnight! It will only grow as you work at it day by day.

DAY 7 - PERSONAL REFLECTION

Write down any questions you have about the Holy spirit:

_____
_____
_____
_____
_____
_____
_____
_____
_____
_____
_____
_____

Spend some time looking at the nine fruit. Can you see if any have become more obvious in your life since becoming a Christian? Thank God for this now.

Now choose 1 or 2 in which you know you still have a lot of growing to do. Spend time asking God to help you to change with the help of His Holy Spirit.

6

The Bible - God's Word

Just as we need food for our bodies, so we need food for our spirits. The Bible is spiritual food that will help us grow and become strong as Christians. It is God's written message to us, to help us learn more about Him and to help us know how to live the Christian life.

You simply cannot survive and grow as a Christian without reading the Bible regularly.

STARTING OUT

DAY 1 - Read 2 Timothy 3:16-17

The word "scripture" refers to the Bible. What do you think "God-breathed" means?

_____
_____
_____

What then should be your attitude to the Bible?

_____
_____
_____

What 4 things is the Bible useful for? (verse 16)

_____
_____
_____

What will reading the Bible do for you? (verse 17)

_____
_____
_____

DAY 2 - Read Psalm 119:9-11

How can you live a pure (holy, good) life? (verse 9)
_____
_____
_____

What does this mean?
_____
_____
_____

What does it mean to "hide God's word in your hearts"? (verse 11)
_____
_____
_____

How will this keep us from sinning?
_____
_____
_____

DAY 3 - Read Psalm 119:12-20

What 2 things did the writer of this Psalm (King David) say he did with the words of the Bible? Explain them both:

VERSE 13:
___

VERSE 15:
___

What does it mean to "neglect" the bible? (verse 16) How might we do this?
___
___
___

What should we ask God for each time before we read the Bible? (verses 12 and 18)
___
___
___

DAY 4 - Read Psalm 119:97-105

How often should we try to think about the word of the Bible? (verse 97)

_____
_____
_____

What will this do for us?

_____
_____
_____

What will reading the Bible do for you? (verse 105) What do you think this means?

_____
_____
_____

DAY 5 - Read Psalm 19:7-11
Fill in this chart:

Verse	What God's Word is Like	What God's Word Does
7:		
7:		
8:		
8:		
9:		
9:		Not Applicable
10:		Not Applicable
10:		Not Applicable
11:		Not Applicable
11:		Not Applicable

DAY 6 - Read James 1:22-25

What are we warned about? (verse 22)
_____
_____
_____

What are we told to do? (in your own words)
_____
_____
_____

What will happen to us if we do this? (verse 25)
_____
_____
_____

DAY 7 - PERSONAL REFLECTION

Write down any questions you have about the Bible:

_____
_____
_____
_____
_____
_____
_____
_____
_____

List here the things that might hinder you from reading the Bible (e.g. distractions):

_____
_____
_____
_____
_____

What do you find hardest about reading the Bible?

_____
_____
_____

When is the best time for you to do it?

_____
_____
_____

Pray now, asking God to help you read the Bible every day. Ask Him to give you the DESIRE to read it.

7

Prayer

If reading the Bible is like eating food, then prayer is like breathing. Prayer is essential for you to survive and grow as a Christian. It is your way of communicating with God. Without it your faith will soon become cold and dead.

God wants you to talk with Him. He wants you to tell Him everything on your heart. He wants you to praise and thank Him. God also wants you to ask Him for things so that He can answer you and help you. What a privilege prayer is! Regular heartfelt prayer, including moment by moment prayers throughout the day should be the highest priority of every Christian.

STARTING OUT

DAY 1 - Read Matthew 6:5-13

How are we to pray? (verses 5-6)

_____
_____
_____

Read the example of prayer that Jesus gives us in verses 9-13. Draw a line from the different kinds of prayer listed below, to the verse number where it is found in this prayer:

Asking for your own needs	Verse 9
Confessing our sins	Verse 10
Asking for help against temptation	Verse 11
Praising God	Verse 12
Praying for God's work in the world	Verse 13

Spend some time praying each of these kinds of prayers now.

DAY 2 - Read Mark 11:22-25

What is Jesus asking you to do when you pray? (verses 22-24)
_____
_____
_____

Does God really want to answer your prayers? (see also Luke 11:9-10)
_____
_____
_____

Does this mean you can get anything you want? Why or why not?
_____
_____
_____

What might stop God listening to your prayers? (verse 25)
_____
_____
_____

DAY 3 - Read Ephesians 6:18

When or how often should we pray?

_____
_____
_____

What should we pray for?

_____
_____
_____

What do you think it means to "pray in the Spirit"?

_____
_____
_____

Make a conscious effort to pray to God all through your day today. You might like to set an hourly reminder in your phone, to remind you to pray each hour of the day – or set a regular alarm on your phone or set your smartwatch to buzz. You will be amazed at what a difference continual prayer makes to your day!

DAY 4 - Read Philippians 4:6-7

What should we be anxious about?
___
___
___

What should we pray about?
___
___
___

To whom should we pray?
___
___
___

How should we pray?
___
___
___

What will happen if we do pray? (verse 7)
___
___
___

DAY 5 - Read Hebrews 10:19-22

What is the "most holy place"? (verse 19)

_____

What gives us the right to "enter" this holy place in prayer?

_____
_____

A priest was someone who spoke to God on behalf of the people. Who is our "great priest" now (and in fact our only priest)? (verse 21)

_____
_____

Because of Jesus, what attitude can we now have when we approach God in prayer? (verse 22)

_____
_____

For context and to help you understand the holy place and priest aspect of this passage, it refers to the Old Testament and how the tabernacle and temple operated. The tabernacle and temple were constructed in such as way as that there were layers of internal spaces. At the centre, was the Holy of Holies, where God dwelt. The chief priest was only permitted to enter the Holy of Holies once per year to make a special offering.

And so the holy place referred to in this passage draws on the history of the nation of Israel and God's relationship with them, mediated by priests. God dwelt among His people in the holy of holies then, with access only to him by priests as intermediaries, yet now dwells amongst us by His Holy Spirit.

DAY 6

The following verses describe Jesus praying on different occasions. Alongside each of the references write down what we can learn from His prayer life:

Mark 1:35   When:
_____
_____

Luke 6:12   How Long:
_____
_____

Luke 5:16   How Often:
_____
_____

Luke 5:16   Where:
_____
_____

What other patterns do you notice?
_____
_____
_____

Did you notice Jesus would pray after healing (Luke 5:16)? He would also pray before miracles (see John 6:11, Matthew 14:23). Maybe keep a note when you read the gospel of when Jesus prayed at the different times and try to incorporate some of those moments into your prayer priorities.

DAY 7 - PERSONAL REFLECTION
Write down any questions you have about prayer.
_____
_____
_____
_____
_____
_____

Many Christians use the **ACTS** formula in their prayer life:
- **A**dorations — praising God for who He is,
- **C**onfession — admitting your sins and asking for forgiveness,
- **T**hanksgiving — thanks for all that God has done for you,
- **S**upplication — requests for yourself and others.

Spend some time praying each of these kinds of prayers now.

Write here the names of people you would like to pray for:
_____
_____
_____
_____

Decide the best time for you to pray each day and write it down. The best time of the day for me to pray is:
_____
_____
_____

Ask God to help you keep this daily appointment, and to remember to pray continually throughout the day.

8

The Church

You cannot exist alone as a Christian: You need other Christians to help you grow in your faith. You are now a part of God's family on earth: the church. The church is not a building - it is the worldwide family of people who are following Jesus. God wants His family to meet together to encourage and help each other, and to work together in telling others about Him.

STARTING OUT

DAY 1 - Read 1 Corinthians 12:12-31

What is another name for this "body"? (see verses 27-28)

_____
_____
_____

How do you become a part of this body? (verse 13) Explain:

_____
_____
_____

Verse 27 is really a summary of this whole passage. In your own words, what is this passage saying?

_____
_____
_____

What does this passage say about your importance in the "body" of Christ and why?

_____
_____
_____

DAY 2 - Read Hebrews 10:24-25

What does this passage say about meeting together?
_____
_____
_____

Why should Christians meet together? (verse 24)
_____
_____
_____

How would meeting together do this?
_____
_____
_____

Why do you think some Christians stop going to church and meeting with other Christians?
_____
_____
_____

STARTING OUT

DAY 3 - Read Acts 2:41-47

This is a description of the very first Christian church. What did they devote themselves to? (verse 42)

___
___

How would you describe their relationship with each other? (verses 44-45)

___
___
___

How often did they meet together? (verse 46)

___
___

In what 2 locations did they meet together? (verse 46)

___
___
___

What should we do if we are going to follow this pattern?

___
___
___

What was the result of all this meeting together and praying? (verse 47)

___
___
___

DAY 4 - Read Ephesians 4:1-13

Although there are many different local churches in the world, in God's eye's how many churches are there? (verse 4)

_____
_____
_____

How should you act towards other Christians? (verses 2-3)

_____
_____
_____

Verse 11 talks about the leaders that God has placed in His church. What is their purpose?

_____
_____
_____

What are Christians meant to do together? (verse 12) Explain:

_____
_____
_____

What 2 things result from us doing these? (verse 13)

_____
_____
_____

DAY 5- Read Ephesians 4:14-16

What will meeting with other Christians protect you from? (verse 14)
_____
_____
_____

Who is the "HEAD" of the church? (verse 15)
_____
_____
_____

Who is the source of our spiritual growth? (verse 16a)
_____
_____
_____

How do we grow as Christians? (verse 16b)
_____
_____

[Note: Verse 16a refers to the first half of the verse. Verse 16b refers to the second half of the verse]

DAY 6 - Read John 17:9-11

This is the prayer Jesus prayed before He left the world. He is praying for His church. What 2 things does Jesus pray for the church in verse 11?

_____
_____

What does it mean to "be one"?

_____
_____
_____

Does this seem important to Jesus?

_____
_____
_____

What things might hinder us being one?

_____
_____
_____

DAY 7 - PERSONAL REFLECTION

Write down any questions you have about the church:

_____
_____
_____
_____
_____
_____
_____
_____
_____
_____
_____
_____

God says it is very important that you meet with other Christians regularly. You should try to attend a church service each Sunday. Many Christians also find great benefit in meeting with others during the week to study the Bible and pray.

What things usually stop you from going to church or perhaps Bible study?

_____
_____
_____

Ask God to help you to be more regular in meeting with His people. If necessary, ask a friend to pick you up each week.

9

Overcoming Temptation

A Christian should have a strong desire to live a holy (sinless) life. We should want this, not in order to "earn" a place in heaven, but in order to please God, who has GIVEN us eternal life as a FREE GIFT.

Yet every Christian is tempted to sin, and at times we give in to that temptation. Satan is at work in this process too, using temptation to try to lure us away from God and make us ineffective as Christians. We have already seen that prayer and Bible study help us to avoid sin. Here are some more important hints to help you overcome temptation.

STARTING OUT

DAY 1 - Read 1 John 2:15-17

From verse 16 list 3 main areas of temptation that we all face, and give at least one practical example of each:

1.
___

2.
___

3.
___

What are we reminded of in verse 17 that should help us resist these temptations?
___

DAY 2 - Read James 1:12-16

What reward is there for those who don't let themselves be led away from God by temptation? (verse 12). Explain what this is:

_____
_____
_____

What is a major source of our temptation? (verse 14)

_____
_____
_____

What is the result of giving in to temptation? (verse 15)

_____
_____
_____

DAY 3 - Read 1 Peter 5:8-10

The devil is another major source of temptation. What is he trying to do when he tempts you? (verse 8). What does this mean?
_____
_____
_____

What are we told to do? (verse 9)
_____
_____
_____

How might we do this?
_____
_____
_____

What are we reminded of that should encourage us? (verse 9)
_____
_____
_____

What does God promise to do? (verse 10)
_____
_____
_____

DAY 4 - Read James 4:7-8

What 2 things are we told to do in verse 7 to overcome temptation? Explain each one:

    1.
_____
_____
_____

    2.
_____
_____
_____

What will happen if we do these 2 things? (verse 7)
_____
_____
_____

What does this tell you about the devil's power compared to the power of Christ within you?
_____
_____
_____

What other things are you told to do in verses 8-10 that might help you overcome temptation?
_____
_____
_____

STARTING OUT

DAY 5 - Read 1 Corinthians 10:12-13

Rewrite in your own words the warning in verse 12:

The most important words in this passage are "God is faithful". What do you think this means?

What 2 important things does God assure us of in regard to temptation? (verse 13)

1.

2.

Does God remove temptation?

DAY 6 - Read Matthew 5:29-30

Jesus did not literally mean for us to physically do this. He was simply illustrating a principle. Explain this principle in your own words:

_____
_____
_____

Read 1 John 1:8-9. When we do give in to temptation and sin, what should we do?

_____
_____
_____

What does God then promise to do?

_____
_____
_____

DAY 7 - PERSONAL REFLECTION

Write down any question you have about overcoming temptation:

___

Write down any temptations that you find hard to resist:

___

What practical things can you do to avoid or minimise these temptations?

___

Spend time asking God to help you overcome these temptations.

10

Sharing Your Faith

Now that you have discovered a relationship with God through Jesus Christ, God doesn't want you to keep it a secret. He wants you to tell others about Jesus and about how they can be forgiven and become His children. Sharing your faith (witnessing) is the most important work you can ever do for God's kingdom. God calls every Christian, no matter how young in the faith, to be a part of His worldwide mission to "seek and save the lost".

STARTING OUT

DAY 1 - Read Mark 5:1-20

The man in this story had been miraculously healed by Jesus. What did Jesus command him to tell his family? (verse 19)

_____
_____
_____

Why do you think Jesus made him go home and tell his family? (Why didn't He let the man stay with Him?)

_____
_____
_____

Verse 20 tells us that the man went around to 10 nearby cities (the "Decapolis") and told many others also. Why do you think he did this? (How must he have felt?)

_____
_____
_____

In what ways are we like this man? What has Jesus done for us?

_____
_____
_____

DAY 2 - Read Matthew 5:14-16

What is Jesus basically saying to us in these verses?
_____
_____
_____

Why should we do this? (verse 16)
_____
_____
_____

How might we put our light under a bowl?
_____
_____
_____

Why might we be tempted to do this?
_____
_____
_____

DAY 3 - Read John 12:42-43

In your own words, why weren't the people willing to say they believed in Jesus?

_____
_____
_____

Read Mark 8:38. What does it mean to be "ashamed" of Jesus?

_____
_____
_____

What warning does Jesus give to such people?

_____
_____
_____

DAY 4 - Read Acts 5:17-42

Read this whole story carefully. In your own words, what did the Apostles (leaders of the early church) say when they were told not to speak about Jesus? (verse 29)

_____
_____
_____

After being flogged (verse 40), how did the Apostles react? (verse 41)

_____
_____
_____

What did they do then? (verse 42)

_____
_____
_____

What lesson does this passage teach us about sharing our faith?

_____
_____
_____

THINK: What kind of persecution am I likely to receive for speaking about Jesus? Am I prepared to even be rejected by my friends? Pray now, asking for strength and boldness.

DAY 5 - Read Acts 18:9-10

These are Jesus' words to the Apostle Paul, but they are also applicable to us. What are we told to do? (verse 9)

_____
_____
_____

Why shouldn't we be afraid? (verse 10)

_____
_____
_____

Read Acts 1:8. What help do we have in our witnessing, and how will He help us?

_____
_____
_____

DAY 6 - Read 1 Peter 3:13-17

Write verse 15 in your own words:
___
___
___

What can we do to "prepare" ourselves to share our faith?
___
___
___

What 2 things should characterise the way we share our faith? (verse 15)
___
___
___

DAY 7 - PERSONAL REFLECTION

Write down any questions you have about sharing your faith:

_____
_____
_____
_____
_____
_____
_____
_____

Write down names of 3 friends you would like to talk to about Jesus:

1. _____

2. _____

3. _____

Pray for them now and ask God to start to open their hearts to His message of salvation. Ask for boldness for yourself and for an opportunity to speak with them about Jesus.

Pray also for God to help you be a good witness to your family.

11

Worshiping God

Worship is our way of telling God how great He is. This should become a part of our daily living and not just something we do one or two days a week. It should also be something we do with our lives as well as our lips. When we live in a way that pleases God, we are worshipping Him. What God is seeking is people who will worship Him with all their hearts and with all their lives.

STARTING OUT

DAY 1 - Read Romans 12:1-2

What "mercy" have we received from God?
_____
_____
_____

Why should this motivate us to worship God?
_____
_____
_____

How does verse 1 say we should worship God?
_____
_____
_____

In your own words, what does verse 2 say we should do? Explain:
_____
_____
_____

DAY 2 - Read Psalm 95:1-7

How would you describe the quality of worship shown in verses 1-2?

_____
_____
_____

What does this suggest about how we should worship God?

_____
_____
_____

List all the things that this passage says we should praise and thank God for:

_____
_____
_____

Write a list of things you can thank God for and do so now in prayer:

_____
_____
_____
_____

DAY 3 - Read Hebrews 13:15-16

Praise is described here as "lips that confess His name". What do you think this means?

_____
_____
_____

Why do you think praise is described here as a "sacrifice"?

_____
_____
_____

How often are we told to offer this sacrifice of praise to God?

_____
_____
_____

Why does it say to do this "through Jesus"?

_____
_____
_____

What does verse 16 say is another way of praising God?

_____
_____
_____

DAY 4 - Read Isaiah 29:13

What is God's criticism of these people's worship?
_____
_____
_____

What does God obviously want our worship of Him to be like?
_____
_____
_____

What can we do to help ourselves worship like this?
_____
_____
_____

DAY 5 - Read Hebrews 12:28-29

Why should we be thankful to God? (verse 28)
_____
_____
_____

How should we worship God?
_____
_____
_____

What do you think this means?
_____
_____
_____

Why should we worship Him like this? (verse 29) Explain:
_____
_____
_____

DAY 6 - Read 1 Corinthians 14:15

What do you think it means to worship God with your spirit?
_____
_____

What do you think it means to worship God with your mind?
_____
_____

What two ways of worshipping God are mentioned?
_____
_____

DAY 7 - PERSONAL REFLECTION

Write down any questions you have about worship:

___

From our study this week, is corporate worship (public worship) a matter of receiving something from God or giving something to God?

___

What things tend to hinder you from worshipping God with all your heart when you meet with other Christians?

___

What practical things can you do to overcome the above?

___

12

Serving God

Now that you are a Christian, your life is no longer your own. You belong to God and have the great privilege of serving Him as your Master. God has given all Christians "spiritual gifts" or special abilities that He wants us to use for the benefit of others. Each of us needs to discover what abilities God has given us and begin to use them to serve Him in the world.

DAY 1 - Read 1 Corinthians 6:19-20

Why is your body called a "temple of the Holy Spirit"?
_____
_____
_____

What does "you are not your own" mean?
_____
_____
_____

What does "you were bought with a price" mean?
_____
_____
_____

If this is true, how then should we live? (verse 20)
_____
_____
_____

DAY 2 - Read 1 Corinthians 12:1-30

What is another name for this "body of Christ"?
_____
_____
_____

In verse 27 what 2 things are you told about your relationship to the body of Christ?

1.
_____

2.
_____

Why does God give Christians spiritual gifts? Whose benefit are they for? (verse 7)
_____
_____
_____

Summarise verses 14- 26 briefly in your own words:
_____
_____
_____
_____
_____

DAY 3 - Read 1 Peter 4:7-11

What is "near"? (verse 7). Explain:
_____
_____
_____

List all the things we are told we should be doing because it is so near:
_____
_____
_____

Why has God given us spiritual gifts? (verse 10)
_____
_____
_____

How should we use our gifts? (verse 11)
_____
_____
_____

DAY 4 - Read James 1:26-27

In your own words, what should true religion result in?

___

What does God obviously want His people to be doing for Him in the world?

___

What are we told to guard against? (verse 27)

___

What does this mean?

___

DAY 5 - Read Luke 17:7-10

In this parable, who does the master represent?
_____
_____
_____

Who does the servant represent?
_____
_____
_____

What does this parable teach us about serving God?
_____
_____
_____

What does it imply about Christians who aren't very faithful in serving God?
_____
_____
_____

DAY 6 - Read Matthew 16:24-27

What does Jesus tell us to do in verse 24?
_____
_____
_____

What do you think this means?
_____
_____
_____

Explain verse 25 in your own words:
_____
_____
_____

Explain the warning in verse 26:
_____
_____
_____

What promises are we given in verse 27?
_____
_____
_____

DAY 7 - PERSONAL REFLECTION

Write down any questions you have about serving God:

_____
_____
_____
_____
_____
_____
_____
_____
_____

God has given you abilities that He wants you to use to help others and to serve Him. Write down any abilities that you know you have:

_____
_____
_____
_____

Can you think of anything you can already start doing to serve God?

_____
_____
_____
_____

Pray now asking for God's strength to serve Him better. Ask Him to help you see new ways of serving Him.

13

Giving To God

As Christians, all things, including our very lives belong to God. This includes our possessions and money. If He is truly our Master, we must learn to use these things the way God wants us to, and not as we would like. In regard to money, many Christians practice 'tithing' (giving one tenth of their income). This was a clear command of God in the Old Testament. How much you give to God's work in the world is strictly between you and God. At the very least, you need to obey the Biblical principles of giving weekly, generously, prayerfully, and in faith, believing that God will meet all your needs.

DAY 1 - Read Acts 4:32-35

What attitude did these early Christians have toward their possessions? (verse 32)

___

What did they sometimes do? (verse 34)

___

Why do you think they did this?

___

What should be your attitude to possessions?

___

Note: Acts describes what happened amongst the people of God in the first Century as they lived together in community. It does not *PRE*scribe how we are to act today, but may give us valuable insight into the heart that God loves to see displayed in His people, and encourage us to emulate that in our context.

DAY 2 - Read Leviticus 27:30-33

In the Old Testament God commanded that everyone should give Him one tenth (a tithe) of their income. (In those days a person's income consisted mainly of produce from the land). Who did this tithe belong to? (verse 30)

_____
_____
_____

Why do you think the tithe was referred to as "holy to the Lord"?

_____
_____

(Note: Holy simply means 'set apart', and in our Christian context "set apart unto God.")

In the Old Testament, part of the tithe was sacrificed (burnt) on an altar to God. The rest was used to support the priests who worked in the temple. In verse 33 the people were commended not to use poor quality animals or produce for their tithe. Why not?

_____
_____
_____

How should we apply this principle to Christian giving today?

_____
_____
_____

DAY 3 - Read Malachi 3:7-10

In this passage God is angry with the people for not giving Him their full tithe. What does God accuse them of in verse 8?

_____
_____
_____

What does He command them to do? (verse 10)

_____
_____
_____

What does He promise if they do this? (verses 10-11)

_____
_____
_____

What principle is there here for us today, particularly for those who say they can't afford to give much to God?

_____
_____
_____

DAY 4 - Read 2 Corinthians 9:6-15

Who should give to God? (verse 7)
___
___
___

How much? (verse 7)
___
___
___

How should we give? (verses 6-7)
___
___
___

How are we NOT to give? (verse 7)
___
___
___

What are we promised? (verse 8)
___
___
___

DAY 5 - Read 1 Corinthians 16:1-2

How often were these early Christians told to give? (verse 2)

_____
_____
_____

The money in this story was being collected for people in need. You may not know of any people, personally, who are in need, but when you give money to your local church, part of that money is used to help the needy.

THINK: How regularly are you giving to God's work in the world? Are you giving weekly as this Bible passage teaches, or is your giving more 'hit and miss'?

You should make a firm commitment to give to God each week. If you are giving to a local church and you are away one week, you should set aside your offering and give it the following week. You may also like to set up a regular recurring payment through your online banking. Think of it as 'Automatic Faithfulness'.

Another principle this passage teaches is making your giving a set percentage of your income (verse 2). Prayerfully consider what percentage you should give and ask God to help you to give it each week.

DAY 6 - Read 1 Corinthians 9:13-14

What is one of the things that our Christian giving is to be used for?
___
___
___

From the words used in verse 14, how important is this to God?
___
___
___

How should this influence our attitude as we give?
___
___
___

DAY 7 - PERSONAL REFLECTION

Write down any questions you have about giving to God:

_____
_____
_____
_____
_____
_____
_____
_____
_____

Spend some time prayerfully considering how much you can give to God's work each week. You might like to fill out the following pledge as a helpful reminder of your commitment to give.

In response to God's love and out of a desire to be obedient in supporting God's work in the world, I pledge, with God's help, to give _____ % of my income, which I estimate to be $_____ each week.

I will today set up a weekly recurring direct deposit through online banking to my churches bank account that reflects my commitment.

14

The Lord's Supper

Jesus said that when we meet together as a Church, we should remember His death on the Cross in a special way. He said that we are to eat bread and drink wine, symbolising His body and blood, as a way of remembering His sacrifice for us. This is a regular, physical reminder of the great price that Jesus paid for our forgiveness.

DAY 1 - Read Luke 22:14-20

What did Jesus say the bread and cup symbolise?

BREAD:
_____
_____
_____

CUP:
_____
_____
_____

What does Jesus ask us to do as we take part in the Lord's Supper? (verse 19)
_____
_____
_____

What, then, do you think you should be doing as the bread and cup are distributed?
_____
_____
_____

DAY 2 - Read 1 Corinthians 11:23-30

In verse 24, what did Jesus say about His body (symbolised by the bread)? Explain:
___
___
___

What does Jesus say about the cup in verse 25?
___
___
___

What do you think this means?
___
___
___

What are we doing every time we take part in the Lord's Supper? (verse 26)
___
___
___

DAY 3 - Read 1 Corinthians 11:23-30

What do you think it means to take part in the Lord's Supper in *"an unworthy manner"*? (verse 27)

_____
_____
_____

What do you think it means to *"examine yourself"* before taking part in communion? (verse 28)

_____
_____
_____

Why do we need to do this? (verses 29-31)

_____
_____
_____

[Note: some Christians in Corinth were falling sick and dying because they were taking part in an unworthy manner].

DAY 4 - Read Matthew 26:26-29

Why did Jesus say His blood was shed? (verse 28)
_____
_____
_____

When did Jesus say He would next take part in this ceremony? (verse 29) Explain:
_____
_____
_____
_____
_____
_____

DAY 5 - Read Acts 2:42

What are the four things these early Christians devoted themselves to?

1. _____

2. _____

3. _____

4. _____

What do you think the "breaking of bread" refers to?
_____
_____
_____

What should it mean for you to be *"devoted"* to *"the breaking of bread"*?
_____
_____
_____

DAY 6 - Read John 6:48-58

Jesus is NOT speaking here about the physical symbols of bread and wine. He is speaking about the spiritual truths that they symbolise. Why do you think Jesus refers to Himself as the *"bread of life"*? (verse 48)

_____
_____
_____

What do you think it means to eat Jesus' body and drink His blood?

_____
_____
_____

In verse 53, Jesus says that unless we eat His body and drink His blood, we cannot inherit eternal life. Why not?

_____
_____
_____
_____
_____
_____

DAY 7 - PERSONAL REFLECTION

Write down any questions you have about the Lord's Supper:

_____
_____
_____
_____
_____
_____
_____
_____
_____
_____
_____
_____
_____
_____

Ask God to give you a proper attitude to the Lord's Supper. The next time you take part in the Lord's Supper, spend some time reflecting on the things you have learnt this week, remembering to confess your sins to the Lord.

END NOTE

Congratulations on completing all 14 weeks of *Starting Out*!

This is the beginning of a lifelong adventure to become more like Jesus. Now that this course is over, continue the daily practices of getting to know God and His character more through reading your bible each day and praying regularly.

There are so many helpful ways to continue to grow in your faith and practice the ways of Jesus. You might like to begin using a daily devotional guide. There are many wonderful ones to choose from. One of them is "The Word For Today" from Vision that you can get delivered to your home for free or to your email each morning – simply visit https://vision.org.au/free/ to sign up.

If you enjoy listening to the spoken word, Alpha have a fantastic audio resource via their app called "Bible in one Year". Search for it in your app store and look for the Red B. This app reads the entire bible to you in one year and is accompanied by devotional thoughts from Nikky Gumble. You can even play it back at a faster speed if the talking is too slow for you.

There are also some great daily devotional books by some fantastic authors. Search online or visit your local Christian bookstore. You might also like to ask other people in your church what devotional books they liked and borrow one from them.

Whether you use a resource like a book, a guide, or an audio app or podcast, the most important thing is to do something. Be intentional about becoming more like Jesus by putting some action alongside your great intentions. Make a real effort towards this life-long goal because that's the reality, it takes time to be transformed. The bible is where it starts however, so keep up the routine of reading it daily. Prayer is also an important daily practice as we have discovered. Continue to pray regularly, and about everything!

END NOTE

Another fantastic way to grow more like Jesus is to do that in community. Not only should you continue to attend a church that regularly preaches the Gospel, but you should also join a small group. Most churches have small groups, as they are the most important place to help you grow. Just like when you met with your discipler or teacher each week during this course, small groups continue that more intimate relationship where you can ask questions, interact, and learn from other Christians. Small groups are also the natural place for pastoral care between the members of the small group. You get to know each other on a deeper level and can be supported and support others through all that life brings together.

And don't forget about finding your fit to serve Jesus with the time, talents, and gifts that He has given you for the church. You are a vital part of His plan to reach the world with the message of Hope that is the Gospel through healthy local churches who love Him, love each other, and love their community.

It's exciting to continue this life-long adventure to become more like Jesus! May God bless you each step of the way, and protect you through the harder times of life, and may you flourish in your faith, hope, and love.

www.ingramcontent.com/pod-product-compliance
Lightning Source LLC
Chambersburg PA
CBHW051951290426
44110CB00015B/2202